First Facts®

MY FIRST SKETCHBOOK

DRAWING FACES

A Step-by-Step Sketchbook

by Mari Bolte
illustrated by Lucy Makuc

CAPSTONE PRESS
a capstone imprint

First Facts are published by Capstone Press,
1710 Roe Crest Drive, North Mankato, Minnesota 56003
www.capstonepub.com

Library of Congress Cataloging-in-Publication Data
Bolte, Mari, author.
  Drawing faces : a step-by-step sketchbook / by Mari Bolte ; illustrated by Lucy Makuc.
      pages cm. — (First facts. My first sketchbook)
  Summary: "Step-by-step instructions and sketches show how to draw a variety of fun
faces"—Provided by publisher.
  ISBN 978-1-4914-0284-9 (library binding)
  ISBN 978-1-4914-0289-4 (eBook PDF)
1. Face in art—Juvenile literature. 2. Drawing—Technique—Juvenile literature. I. Makuc,
Lucy, illustrator. II. Title.
  N7573.3.B65 2015
  743.4'2—dc23   2014013814

Editorial Credits
Juliette Peters, designer; Katy LaVigne, production specialist

Photo Credits
Capstone Studio: Karon Dubke, 5 (photos); Shutterstock: Azuzl (design element),
Kalenik Hannah (design element), oculo (design element)

Printed in the United States of America in North Mankato, Minnesota.
042014   008087CGF14

Table of Contents

Sketching Smiles 4

Guard On Duty 6

Outdoor Girl 8

Goofy Guy.................................. 10

Friendly Fireman 12

Elegant Lady.............................. 14

Scowling Sweetie 16

Scared!.................................... 18

First Mate................................. 20

Luau Lad 22

Read More.................................24

Internet Sites 24

Sketching Smiles

Masks, goggles, frowns,
  and mouths that say, "Boo!"
Sketching faces is fun,
  and learning to draw is too!

Don't scowl if you don't know where to begin. This book is just for you. Follow these tips and the simple steps on each page. You'll be drawing toothy, frowny, and funny faces in no time.

TIP 1 **Draw lightly.** You will need to erase some lines as you go, so draw them light.

TIP 2 **Add details.** Little details, such as smile lines or hair curls, are a nice touch.

TIP 3 **Color your drawings.** Color can make a bright, smiling drawing even happier!

You won't need a helmet or crown.
But you will need some supplies.

drawing paper

eraser

pencil

pencil sharpener

colored pencils
or markers

Sharpen your pencils, and get ready to draw
all the faces you see. It will be a silly, screaming,
smiling time!

Guard on Duty

Under their bearskin hats, Queen's Guard soldiers have a tough job. They protect all the royal palaces in England. Draw one of these serious soldiers.

Final

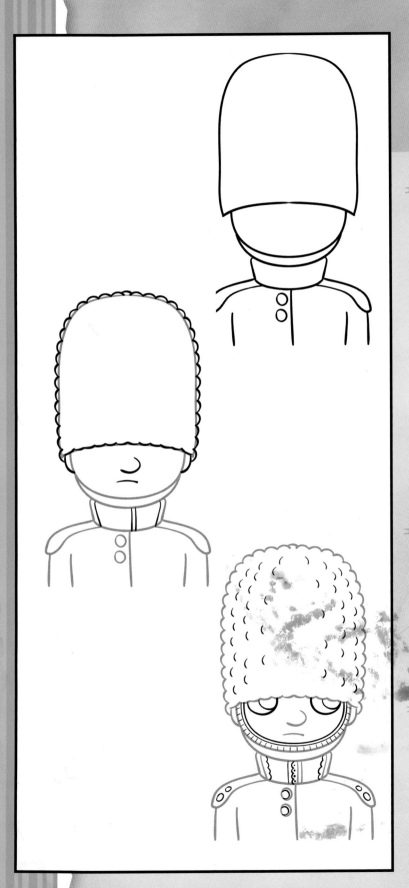

Draw a tall mound shape for the guard's hat. Add two smaller half circles underneath. Draw a square with rounded corners for a neck. Add detail lines to fill in the guard's shoulders and begin the guard's jacket.

Don't Forget!
Erase lines that go under something else. For example, erase the curved line you drew for the hat in Step 1.

Add a scalloped line around the hat. Use curved lines for ears. Draw detail lines for the guard's nose, mouth, and neck decoration.

Add two half circles for eyes. Draw smaller half circles for pupils. Sketch many small detail lines for the hat and the rest of the guard's uniform.

Outdoor Girl

This little sweetie is ready to hit the slopes, go snowshoeing, or build a snowman. Draw her surrounded by snowflakes!

Final

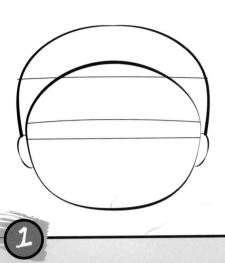

1 Draw a circle for a head. Add a larger half circle. Draw two straight lines at the bottom of the half circle. Add another line in the middle of the half circle. Draw two curved lines for ears.

2 Draw a scalloped line around two of the straight lines. Add two pointed lines for the snowboarder's hair. Use two circles for eyes and a curved line for a nose.

3 Draw more pointed lines for the rest of the snowboarder's hair. Add two circles for pom-poms. Give the eyes more character by drawing almond shapes over the circles. Don't forget to add a smile.

4 Draw more scalloped lines on the fluffy part of the hat. Add scalloped lines around the pom-pom circles. Draw more detail lines for hair.

Goofy Guy

What kinds of funny faces can you make? Get creative and draw them all on this goofy-looking guy.

Final

1

Draw an oval for a head. Add two half circles for ears. Trace a line around the head from ear to ear. Add a slightly scalloped line for a neck.

2

Add three large pointed lines and two small pointed lines for hair. Draw two circles for eyes. Add a long curved line and two smaller curved lines for a mouth. Use curved and straight lines for the boy's sweater.

3

Draw more pointed lines for hair. Add a long half circle and a detail line for a tongue. Add two curved lines for teeth, and a third for a nose. Sketch curved detail lines for eyebrows. Use two short lines for the boy's body.

4

Add curved lines to the sweater. Draw two curved lines inside each ear. Add a second curved line to the eyebrows. Detail lines finish the eyes, nose, and mouth.

Friendly Fireman

Rescuing cats. Putting out fires. Saving lives.
Firemen are great—and they're great to draw too!

Final

1 Draw a large bell shape. Draw three curved lines across the bell.

2 Join the two bottom two curved lines in a point. Draw a square shape above the center of the top curved line. Add the number 1. Use curved lines to draw the outline of the fireman's face.

3 Add a smaller rectangle around the number 1. Sketch scalloped lines for hair. Add detail lines to the top and sides of the helmet. Draw more detail lines for eyes, eyebrows, and a nose.

4 Draw larger eye circles. Add more scalloped lines for hair. Use additional detail lines for the mouth, eyebrows, and number square.

Elegant Lady

She's dressed up to go anywhere! After drawing her face, why not add the rest of her outfit?

Final

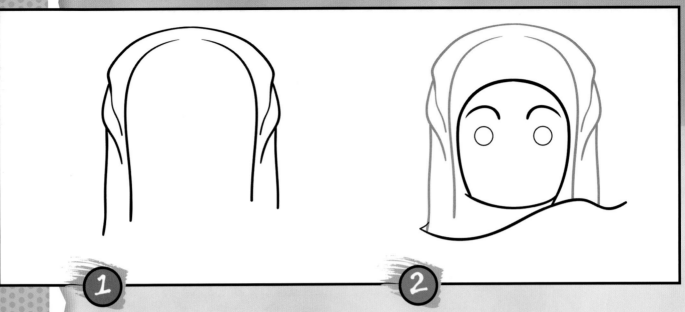

1

Draw an upside-down curved line. Add straight and curved lines around the curve.

2

Add an oval with a flat bottom. Draw a curved line below the straight lines from Step 1. Add two curved lines for eyebrows and two circles for eyes.

3

Draw darker curved lines around the eye circles. Add short and long curved lines for the scarf. Use short curved lines for the nose and eyelashes, and a straight line for a mouth.

4

Use a short, straight line for the bridge of the nose. Use curved lines around the mouth for lips. Add small curved lines for eyelids. Use scalloped detail lines to decorate the scarf.

Scowling Sweetie

What do you think could be bothering this little girl? Draw her scowling face—then try making her happy!

Final

1

Draw a circle for a head, and a straight line right below. Add smaller circles for eyes and half-circles for ears. Add two curved lines above the circle. Draw a long curved line across the forehead and two smaller curves toward each ear. Add more curved lines above the eyes for eyebrows.

2

Add dark curved lines around the eyes. Draw small circles and detail lines for earrings and hair decorations. Add two bell shapes for the girl's shoulders.

3

Add long, swooping lines for the pigtails. Use straight and curved lines for arms. Pointed lines add detail to the girl's bangs, and curved lines form her shirt collar. Add a little curved line for her nose and small detail lines inside her ears.

4

Sketch more long, swooping lines to the girl's hair. Add lines across the bell shapes to give her shirt cuffs and curved lines to finish her arms. Add marks for freckles and small scalloped lines for her shirt collar. Add her frown to complete her sour look.

Scared!

This guy has seen something super scary! First draw his scared face. Then draw what you think scared him.

Final

1 Draw an oval for a head. Add curved and spiked lines for hair. Add a large curved line for shoulders and a smaller curved line for a neck.

2 Add straight lines for shirt sleeves and arms. Draw an oval shape for an ear. Then add more curved and spiked hair lines.

3 Draw two circles for eyes. Add a square with three curved corners and one pointed corner. Sketch two half circles for teeth and a tongue. Add curved detail lines for the shirt design.

4 Use dark lines to add eyebrows. A number 2 shape will give detail to the ear. Add a curved line and dot for a nose. Use detail lines to add bottom teeth and a neck, and to finish the eyes.

First Mate

This pirate is ready to sail to the ends of the Earth. Use speech bubbles to give him a voice. Is his favorite phrase, "Ahoy, matey!" or is a simple, "Arrrrr!" more his style?

1 Draw an oval shape. Draw a straight line across the top part of the oval. Use an upside-down question mark for his nose.

2 Add a half circle for an ear. Draw curved lines for a mustache. Then sketch a few detail lines across the top of his head.

3 Use two curved lines for an earring. Add scalloped lines on his mustache, hair, and bandana knot. Use two curved lines for an eyebrow.

4

Add a scalloped line all the way across his chin. Add more scalloped lines for the top of his beard. Curved and straight lines add part of his eye patch and bandanna.

5

Use a half circle for the rest of his eye patch. A circle and a dot make up his good eye. Use a backward 5 shape to add detail to his ear and a little pointed line for the rest of his bandanna.

Final

Luau Lad

This happy lad is ready to say, "Aloha 'Oe!" Do the hula with your pencil and draw the best luau ever.

Final

1 Draw an oval for a head. Add a curved line across the top. Add a half oval underneath. Use curved and straight lines for ears, eyes, and a smile.

2 Use leaf shapes to fill in his lei and crown. Add more curved lines for the rest of his smile, his eyes, and his nose.

3 Continue adding leaf shapes. Use curved lines to add more detail to his eyes and mouth.

4 Add curved lines inside each leaf for texture. Add two thin ovals for eyebrows. Use curved and straight lines for his neck, shoulders, and body. Draw very small scalloped lines for hair.

Read More

Bergin, Mark. *It's Fun to Draw Pirates*. It's Fun to Draw. New York: Sky Pony Press, 2014.

Curto, Rosa M. *Fun and Easy Drawing Storybook Characters*. Fun and Easy Drawing. Berkeley Heights, N.J.: Enslow Publishers, 2013.

Guillain, Charlotte. *Get Drawing!* Dream It, Do It! Chicago: Capstone Raintree, 2014.

Internet Sites

FactHound offers a safe, fun way to find Internet sites related to this book. All of the sites on FactHound have been researched by our staff.

Here's all you do:

Visit *www.facthound.com*

Type in this code: 9781491402849

Super-cool stuff!

Check out projects, games and lots more at
www.capstonekids.com